THE SKY WILL HOLD

Elizabeth Hazen

Riot in Your Throat
publishing fierce, feminist poetry

Copyright © Elizabeth Hazen 2025

No part of this book may be used or performed without written consent from the author, if living, except for critical articles or reviews.

Hazen, Elizabeth.
1st edition.
ISBN: 979-8-988-9898-9-9

Cover Art: Markus Spiske (unsplash.com)
Cover Design: Kirsten Birst
Book Design: Shanna Compton
Author Photo: E. Brady Robinson

Riot in Your Throat
Arlington, VA
www.riotinyourthroat.com

for my parents, who taught me to look deeper

CONTENTS

PART 1

9 Approximations
10 Second Marriage
11 Hell's Half Acre
13 Margin of Error: a Glose after "Mon Semblable" by Stephen Dunn
15 Luminosities
16 Panic
17 Making Teeth
19 The Thing with Feathers
20 Fable
22 Horses
24 When Your Mother Died, I Drank Again
26 Sensory Integration
28 Risk Assessment
30 Real Estate for the Blended Family (or What I Learned from Zillow)
32 Lady Tremaine's Defense
34 The Juniper Tree
36 Dreaming Sisyphus Happy
37 After Reading *Restricted Movement* by Traci O'Dea
38 Mercy
40 Whelm
41 Sheep Mountain Table
42 Woman at Forty-Five

PART II

47 A Kind of Magic
49 On the Precipice
51 Glose for my Son, after Bishop's "In the Waiting Room"

53	September
54	Epiphany in the Badlands
55	First Love at Four Corners
57	Elegy: Shiprock 2021, with My Teenage Son
59	On a Spring Day, My Son Comes to Me Despairing
60	Glose for Sarah
62	Late September in Druid Hill Park
63	Dance Class
64	Listening to Spotify on the Ride to School, Winter 2021
66	Pathetic Fallacy
67	The Deer
69	Glose for Fathers
71	Waiting for Bats
73	Retreat
74	Glose After Seshadri's "Cliffhanging"
76	Driving My Son Home from the Tattoo Parlor
78	I don't believe in magic
79	Such Wonders
84	Acknowledgments
85	Thanks
86	About the Author
87	About the Press

PART 1

APPROXIMATIONS

The sun is not on fire after all;
nothing burns. Protons smash to make a gaseous

mass of heat, but without flame. All these years
I've had it wrong, like when my anger wasn't

anger, rather fear mixed up with loneliness—
but I was talking about the sun, the nuances

of burning, the stories we learn as children:
bulls charge if they see red, the moon alone

controls the tides, and Twinkies last forever.
Didn't we all wait for watermelons to bloom

in our bellies? Bank on the belief that effort
yields reward? Doesn't your name, too, sound

like a foreign language? Look at us: barefaced,
slouching through middle age. I wouldn't say

the birds here sing so much as shriek. I wouldn't
trust myself to say a thing, betrayed as I am

by language. This sun that burns us isn't fire,
but look at us: our cheeks flush just the same.

SECOND MARRIAGE

1.
Our bedroom light projects a screen
against the backyard trees, green-

black leaves rustling. Velvet dark shushes
like Miss Clavel. A condenser hisses,

and far away fireworks or gunshots pop.
The stand of locust trees plots

its next move. I tell myself I'm safe.
I tell myself stories about force fields and fate—

as if any of us get what we deserve—
and if we did, could we live with what we've earned?

2.
Even now, lost in separate reveries,
me in the winking darkness, darkest memories

almost lost in shadows of the looming trees,
and you in the kitchen oblivious to me,

grinding tomorrow's coffee, tracking down
your wayward son, I know how close to drowning

I have been. I am grateful for the air
up here, the fox's scream, the firefly's flare,

and you, your puttering like a well-loved song.
I never thought I'd live this long.

HELL'S HALF ACRE

The day we drove across Wyoming, I pinned
my fears on home; your children's resentments
followed me west, shadowing me like bad weather.

The geology itself was an aftermath,
wind-scarred and cragged like an enduring face—
that kind of beautiful. From Riverton

to Hell's Half Acre, I brooded; your confusion
blurred the periphery. I wish I could
explain my anger, the menace of my dread.

I almost missed the sign which, along with chain-
link fencing, was all that set the place apart from the miles
we'd already driven. So much spectacular

sameness begins to numb a person. The brittle
plains were savaged by chasms, cratered like
movie-set moons. I have been a stranger

in every house I've entered. Time reveals
itself in lines: stripes on a cliff face, rings
in a tree trunk, wrinkles across my brow,

cracks in our house's foundation. We walked
the fence in opposite directions. You took
a phone call from your daughter, so I kept

my distance jealously. The visit lasted
no more than ten minutes. The only photograph
I took is a closeup of the fence, the badlands

beyond a smudge. Back in the car I wanted
to say something redeeming, but you touched
my arm so gently, I was mute. I'm sorry.

I see only edge and threat surrounding me—
a flawed perspective—in truth the rocks
are soft enough to crumble in my hands.

MARGIN OF ERROR: A GLOSE AFTER "MON SEMBLABLE" BY STEPHEN DUNN

> *. . . but those words unsaid*
>
> *poison every next moment.*
> *I will try to disappoint you*
> *better than anyone ever has . . .*

Is there any way around the failure
of language? I say, *I can't live without you*,
but most days I exist for hours
alone: I read the news, drink coffee, write
poems—and you are at the office or riding your bike—
or even if we are together, absently making the bed,
you are not exactly with me, but
parallel. *You are everything to me* is also not
quite right, naïve words of a romantic or newlywed—
but those words unsaid

are the glaring rectangle of paint
where a picture used to hang.
What can I say to clarify? Sometimes
I don't like how easily I survive
your absence. I breathe in and out;
sometimes I even sleep better alone. I resent
my self-sufficiency—and yours. We lived
without each other for decades. I feel
more present now; I don't let my discontent
poison every next moment.

I'm sorry I don't reveal myself
one mask at a time; I grace you
with no such order, but I do reveal myself

in other ways. So do you. You set
your jaw and look away
when you are angry. I do that, too:
turn stone. But in the center of each of us
there is fire. I hate that neither of us will ever feel
the other's burning—just embers, residue.
I will try to disappoint you

only enough to remind you that my deficiencies,
fewer since knowing you, are my own.
I'm no longer trying to escape
myself or disappear into someone else;
words fall short. *You saved me*
sounds dramatic. *You show me myself as
someone you would choose* is close. *Of everything,
I choose you* is true. You give me
more than anyone ever has,
better than anyone ever has.

LUMINOSITIES

Luminosity is more than light:
it's radiant power over time,

a lasting glow like Nordic summers,
that reedy yellow stretching thin

even over nighttime hours. Distance
is more than physical space. You feel it

in a shoulder curved away, the tensing
of a jawline. Unlike stars, we choose

what to reveal: a woman fading
into wallpaper or her smile

bright as planets. Once I caught you
seeing me across a crowded party.

Neither of us moved, but energies
shifted. Seeing your face aglow,

my own reciprocated light.
What I don't know could fill galaxies,

but I've seen magic in the space that lies
between knowledge and belief.

PANIC

No purpose to my days, I set small fires
to pass the time. The hours

flex their muscles. The flint
barely cracks a spark, a wink, a glint

that goes out too soon most times—
but when it does catch, the flames

devour themselves, growing great
with their own devastation. Fate

is just unintended consequences—
let one ember ignite, and all sense

transmutes to ruin: a banshee
with curled fingernails; a gorgon, green

and merciless; a girl with a loaded gun
trapped inside a woman with her tongue

cut out. Under my skin, they pace,
rattle me, give color to my face.

MAKING TEETH

My mother didn't have a name for it,
but Sue's mom called it "mommy drag"—not just

the pantyhose and painted face she wore
to pick up kids from school or playdates, but

the whole charade of niceties. My mother
spent her days in sweatpants writing, but changed

into a dress before my father came
back home. I thought such transformations part

and parcel of a woman's lot, the people
we became in public like costumes concealing

our true selves from the world, like the hollow book
where my mother stored her pearls, hidden in plain sight.

Sue and I walk through the woods, smoking weed
like teenagers, but unafraid of getting caught:

middle-aged women are innocuous as moss.
When we become invisible, will we

be able to stop hiding? Give up the mores
of our mothers, unclench our smiles? Sue's mother called it

"making teeth"; my mother's version, "grin and bear it,"
smiles accessories like earrings or silk scarves.

Making teeth, I say out loud, the words themselves
like gnashing, a sinking into things, vicious

as the jaws of an angry dog, cold as forceps,
speculums—the tools of turning women

inside-out. The words are razors in my mouth:
make teeth make teeth make teeth make teeth make teeth.

THE THING WITH FEATHERS

I do not recognize my face, fallen
as it is with age, but I know I have become
the woman rolling bits of bread between

arthritic fingers, tossing them to the murder
at her feet. The crows' eyes are not black as I once
believed, but brown so rich their pupils almost

disappear. I've learned such details matter.
Strangers pass but pay me no mind; I've sat
so long on this bench, I'm invisible to them,

but a crow approaches me, dropping a pebble
from her beak. I've spent my whole life waiting
for this offering. I guard it like a relic.

FABLE

The sky has been falling for decades, crushing us
under its weather. We've had no choice but to dig

our own graves, places to hide from the havoc
coming down. My father taught me how to disengage

rock from cliff face, how to clean surfaces
with my tongue, but nothing about putting things

to rights. Time is a shoe sinking beneath
the surface of a pond, green film gulping

it under. Giving a thing a name is not
the same as substance. We grasp for words, for air,

for heaven which will fall and crush us, but
for which we nonetheless keep reaching. We call

to mothers who forgot us years ago.
The sky falls and presses us down, gravity

stronger than the arms that hold us, the gruff
Hold still—the force like the will we use each day

to carry on. I see the light shifting;
our axis has tilted. The sky falls like a hatch

to seal us in; we define our personal spaces,
stock our bunkers, shelter in place. The sky

is an illusion, after all. There's solid
ground and air we breathe (if we are lucky

enough to breathe unhindered) and atmosphere
we call sky, but the idea of *blue* is just

reflection. The idea that there's a limit
to the damage we can do is myth. Our greed

will bring the whole world crashing down
and still we will insist *It's only weather.*

HORSES

Tonight, your side of the bed is empty.
I drink when you're away, cradling the bottle,

my tenuous secret. In the movie I'm half-
watching, dusk shadows the hero as he parks

and jumps a fence, approaching a huddle of horses.
They don't skitter or complain. They seem to be

expecting him. They let him rub their noses.
Before we married, we hiked lava fields

in Iceland, a landscape marbled black and green,
cold gusts pushing us ahead. I was happy.

Near that mossy path behind a gate, horses
grazed daintily. The blonde one held your gaze.

You combed her mane with your fingers, your gentleness
striking, your eyes wet. I took a photograph.

It was then I knew your kindness would undo me,
but in the darkness of our bedroom now,

I am alone. I know you will return,
but somehow those sweet days of early love

don't feel like mine to keep. On screen a sudden
blast, fists of orange flexing against dark sky.

The horses scatter. The man runs toward his car,
astonished by the blaze. I've lost the plot,

but understand with certainty, my love,
that you are the horses, nosing grass in easy

moonlight, while I am the exploding car:
a hazard to flee and gape at from afar.

I want to warn you: get out while you can.
I want to keep you forever in my burning.

WHEN YOUR MOTHER DIED, I DRANK AGAIN
for GWP

You leave to tend to her affairs, and I'm tossing empty
bottles in the neighbor's bin before
you've had a chance to miss my fingers
pressed against your back, the way we collapse
into each other, exploding matter birthing stars.
Before you even reach your mother's

house, I've bought another fifth. Like my mother,
I drink alone. You enter the near-empty
house, sort through what's left of her things. The stars
are brighter where you've gone; I'm jealous before
I even see the photographs, time-lapse
records of how far away you are. Three fingers

in a juice glass later, I'm texting you, my fingers
shooting off frantic messages. Your mother
died, but I am falling, calling out, mid relapse,
desperate for you, desperate for a fix that will empty
the raging clutter in my head. You've heard it before,
my diatribes, excuses. I used to say the stars

aligned for us, but what do I know of stars?
They are celestial fists flexing fingers
of light that disappear years before
we see them. What if I'm a curse? Fate is the mother
of all lies, beguiling us with happy endings, our empty
mouths gaping. My love, what if you mistook lapsed

reason for attraction? Most addicts relapse
more than once—we've all seen the tabloid stars,

contrite posturing all the way to rehab, empty
promises echoing. Between urge and action my fingers
drum surfaces like busy machinery, the mother-
board circuitry lit up. If I've said all this before

it's because it happened over and over before
we met, only then I hid my shame in the laps
of men who never learned my name. Your mother
disappointed, too, erratic with anger. The stars
frown at my selfishness. I thought I was empty
of the past, but I watch it, shamed, through my fingers.

Why can't those years before we met fade like dying stars,
elapse into ether? At the funeral home you finger
locks of your mother's hair until your heart is empty.

SENSORY INTEGRATION
after Emily Dickinson

I am out with lanterns looking for myself.
The lanterns are unlit. I've burned myself out.

The sky turns blue as periwinkles. Blossoms
litter the too-green grass like confetti,

petals pink as a dolled-up baby girl.
It's all too sweet to be real. You need to be

outside in the dank spring air to smell the vulgar
pear blossoms, the rot that trails new life: shed

skins and earthworms, their copper scent, writhing
on pavement after rain. I can't remember

belonging in this body. I flow over
the brim of myself. I brim with memories

of what might have been. Remember when the kids
were young? Loss begets loss as time moves on.

Your fingertips trace questions on my knee.
I stiffen, pull away. All I say out loud

is *sure* and *yes* and *I'm okay*, but muscle
memory hammers *No no no*. It isn't you,

my love. The unremembered details still
menace my body. No matter how gentle

your touch, I feel myself besieged, a child
seeking cover, cowering in this skin.

RISK ASSESSMENT

1.
I wake at five, no need for an alarm,
powered by routine: check the scale, brush teeth,
drink coffee, feed the cat. These motions are
salvation, boxes I can check, safe havens
to protect me from a universe of threat.

2.
I soothe myself with stories: *I am a princess
trapped inside a castle. I am the castle
made of stone. I am thorny vines that hold
the castle hostage. I am the scythe that cuts
away the vines.* How do I disappear
when everyone is looking? How do I
disappear when nobody is looking?

3.
My keys are in my hand three blocks before
I reach my car. The old-milk smell of lunchrooms
follows me down the alleyway from work,
sending me back to playground scuffles, violence
in me even then. Over the city lurks
an orange haze, wildfire clouds blown south.

4.
There's no such thing as isolated incidents;
life ripples out, pond water disturbed by stones.

5.
A month ago, a mourning dove smashed into
our bedroom window. She staggered in circles,
stunned, before flying away. Even now
I see the smudge of her outstretched wings on the glass,
a vague impression echoing the crash.

REAL ESTATE FOR THE BLENDED FAMILY (OR WHAT I LEARNED FROM ZILLOW)

The houses are photographed with light in mind:
The sun, they say, *is shining here*. The filter

hints at lemons: fresh laundry on a quaint
old line. The "den" becomes the "family room"

where we'd play rummy and watch TV, the square
footage enough to hold all our misgivings.

Here I'd be the kind of wife who does not feel
resentment. I'd have a thousand cheeks to turn,

and I'd never hold a grudge. Here I'd become
a Carol or June, selfless and well-groomed.

When I moved in, we built new walls to make
more rooms, but Frost was right—we gave offense:

new walls created doors for them to slam.
When your children left, I whispered my objections,

their fury like a suitcase threatening
to burst. I want a house that holds no past,

the gate unlatched, inviting us to enter
well-lit, neutral rooms where we'd feng shui

the bitterness, hide scars under photographs
of us together, smiling. But in this house,

I am a ghost: invisible, unwanted.
Come Back and *Sorry* strain my throat. I want

to fix this—douse this fire spitting: *Good.*
Get out, my apron starched to armor. No

recipe can quell the acid rising
in our throats. Sometimes I dream of gardens—

that same dirt they kick from their cleats could feed us,
grow something to sustain us. But it's winter.

The ground is cold, and I dare not leave this room;
I want to want to fix this—to love them

after all—but in here I am safe. I've space
to rage and pace, dark curtains and a door.

LADY TREMAINE'S DEFENSE
Cinderella's Stepmother Speaks

I too was steeped in kindness once, dripping
good intentions. Once upon a time, I fed

sick neighbors with homemade soup, smiled at strangers
without guile—but kindness cannot feed us,

nor—despite what poets say—can love. Lies
we were told as girls kept us docile as toy

poodles, pliable as putty. It's true,
I threw her heaps of washing, plucked the buttons

from my dress, insisting, *Fix this*. But what else
should I have done? It was not cruelty, but

common sense: she was too soft, and we all know
what happens to pretty girls who trust too much.

Once, even I fell for a man. He left me
with two daughters and a scalding shame: *How could*

I be so stupid? After that, I took
what I could get; time thickened my skin.

It's true, I do feel jealousy—her beauty
is a cruelty in itself, her youth a ceaseless

taunting that deepens my own creases, turns
downward the arc of my lips. Logic falls

victim to the torrent of my rage, but
shouldn't she thank me, after all? I taught

her what it is to be unwanted, forced
her to find strength she never would have known.

I was not always of this mind. For a time,
I smiled easily, threw crumbs to the birds

that love her so, waiting for a man to take
notice. I'm sure I see her smirk at me,

eyes slit to bright blue gashes. When no one else
is watching, she baits me, shaking her flaxen locks,

her translucent skin a mirror that distorts:
it tells me I'm a monster. What kind of world

would fault me for surviving, for passing on
my legacy like a coat of arms? If we were men

they would promote me to General, praising
my sangfroid, my strategy. Instead, I'm cast

as petty and mean, she as my faultless prey.
Glass slippers, glass ceilings—I'd like to shatter

everything that breaks, but with my luck she'd cut
her feet, for which I'd also suffer blame.

THE JUNIPER TREE

The Grimms tell of a magic tree, a murder,
and a bird who sings of the evil stepmother

who could not see beyond her fear that love
is a zero-sum game: more children mean less bread

to go around and husbands only have
two hands, one heart. It's greed that drives *her* cruelty.

I know nothing but abundance, no need
to vie for food or love, but sometimes what

a person feels becomes a kind of truth.
I fear my stepchildren see behind my smile

as I take stock, hear the insecurity
tight in my throat, my saccharin tone like arsenic.

In the story, she cooks her stepson into stew,
then feeds her husband flesh of his flesh, gristle

catching in his teeth. He asks for seconds, clueless
as a stone. My husband doesn't see the way

his children stiffen at my presence, doesn't
feel, as I do, the slap of their shut doors.

The boy's bones, interred beneath the juniper,
give rise to an exquisite bird who sings

of the stepmother's evil deeds. All I did was fall
in love with a man who loved a wife before me.

If I'm inclined to violence, I turn
it on myself: I am the bird who drops

a millstone on the bitch's head, restoring
the boy to life. I am the millstone, pale

and hard, a slab marking the grave of a family
that predates me. I am the birdsong, brightly

casting accusations, confessing all
my ugliness in a single melodious hymn.

DREAMING SISYPHUS HAPPY

I'm in a used bookshop: creaky wood floors
riddled with splinters, coat of dust, spider webs
and musk of mildewed pages. The architecture of dreams:

stairways going up take me down to the street
and the inside is far bigger than the storefront
should allow. I'm late again for something, though

I've no idea for what, and I drop a box
of nails I didn't know I held. Uncanny
light of sunsets glows gold and pink. As soon

as I plink the last nail in the box, they all
spill out again. I use my hand as a broom,
then grasp fistfuls of nails, ignoring the pricks

in my palm, but again and again they fall.
The light has darkened into that shadowy blue
of dusk. Wherever I was meant to be,

I'm far past being late. The shopkeeper
frowns at me, heaving proprietary sighs.
I rush to gather all the nails, but time

is running out. I wake, my fingers twitching.
I have no box of nails. I've lost nothing
so must have nothing to recover, but

nonetheless I feel bereft. I want to stay
in the moment when I've plucked up the last nail,
before they scatter again like shiny seeds.

AFTER READING *RESTRICTED MOVEMENT* BY TRACI O'DEA

When I opened my eyes the tree branches were snakes
with green tongues blossoming from their hissing mouths
until I blinked and they were only limbs

bothered by the breeze. The addict stays an addict
in the book I read last night. Over and over
he overdoses, but he doesn't die.

His daughter writes his illness in blank verse,
the iambs forcing order. I understand
the need to shape what we cannot control.

Universes grow from tiny parts, the rhythm
of my husband's voice reminding me to breathe.
The world is rife with complicated things.

As a child I found a haven in our pine tree,
the hollow space inside the lower branches
like a cave, the floor of needles soft as moss.

From this lair, I watched the neighborhood unseen.
What I mean is I have always found a way
to hide. The addict stays an addict, keeping

bottles deep in drawers. The allure in part
is secrecy. When I thought the trees were snakes
I wasn't scared so much as mesmerized.

MERCY

1.
Clouds like gauze wrap the wounded moon.
The breathing my doctor taught me fails

to soothe, but Xannies slacken me,
my own weight like a man's insistent hands.

Remember cigarettes, the ashy burn?
This finger down my throat has become

untenable. I decline all incoming calls.
Your years on the farm taught you

efficiencies of letting go: penetrating
captive bolt or gunshot to the back

of the skull—no passion in such release,
no question of right or wrong.

2.
On the trail behind the city zoo
a wounded squirrel trembles. You finish

her off with your boot heel, but I am too
far gone to hear her crack, just as when

my father wrapped our hamster, disfigured
with tumors, in a plastic bag. I hid

in the closet until he brought the hammer
down and called me back to bury her.

3.
There are places from which we can't
come back; we linger like ghosts

or fingerprints. So much of me is somewhere
else, I don't think I'm here at all.

WHELM

Year after year, I am underdressed, uneasy
as an uninvited party guest. I buy

lipsticks that sit in a drawer, little tubes
like shotgun shells. I eye my reflection in each

window I pass, generally discouraged.
At home, we watch the tiny buds sway at the tops

of the locust trees. You recognize the set
of my jaw and touch my arm, undoing me.

My tears are ugly and undignified,
but you stay. The world outside our world is rife

with unsolicited advice, insistent
voices spewing sentiment and recipes.

This is what I fear: the too-muchness of living,
the chasm of my own need. The unreal colors

outside fade when a cloud obscures the sun.
April is always colder than I expect;

I pull sundresses from the cedar chest,
but for weeks they hang unworn like pastel ghosts.

SHEEP MOUNTAIN TABLE

We hang our legs over edge of scarp, eating
instant noodles, shout into the canyon
to bandy with our echoes. I love the bristling

grasses, sandstone sea, this landscape vast as
loneliness. We sleep little. Each gust thunders
against the tent, jolting us from half-dreams,

and when the wind dies down, the enormity
of quiet is like being underwater.
Below us, hoodoos like rows of jagged teeth.

You know that feeling when the highway opens
at the end of a traffic jam? Like magic, cars
disperse and you can speed away, renewed

and optimistic. That's what this is like.
Back home, my worries wait like unpaid bills.
I know you've seen the wilderness inside me,

insecurities sharp and hard as gravel spat
from spinning tires. But here my fears quiet.
I let you hold my hand, hold me here with you.

We brew coffee in the early dawn. I want
to carry this space inside me like a breath,
like the morning light transforming dull clay

into a vibrancy of ochre and rust.
We leave no trace, but still I see us there
joyfully casting words into the void.

WOMAN AT FORTY-FIVE

Time is a stepmother staking her claim, establishing
boundaries, getting her house in order. Time

is a bully with violent fists; for years I turned
my pockets out for her. But these days I lie

in bed watching the sun come up, watching
the deer who nibble at the brush out back.

Dawn transforms the sky from black to bluish-white.
The trees, so narrow and erect, could be bars.

A clump of green and gold balloons has been stuck
in the branches of a locust tree for years now,

Mardi Gras-colored mylar shimmering
against the washed-out world. I didn't write

a thing all week, but watched vibrations of
the leafless trees. The hours ask nothing of me.

For years I waited for a sign—directive
or disaster—to dictate what came next, but time

is patient, has nowhere else to be. In the mirror,
cruel cliché, a stranger with dark circles,

a weariness set deep behind the eyes.
And what of success? I've no status to report.

I've been lucky my whole life and still this
disappointment. Some cultures read the map

of aging faces with respect; in ours
I'll fade out, a ghost before I've died. No matter.

Wait long enough and everything will change.
Wait long enough and everything will circle

back to what it was before you got here.
The trees know nothing of striving, of titles

or commendations. A month from now leaves
will fill my view with verdancy. The sun

burns on its own power, immovable
and fierce. Time is indifferent as a river.

Let it smooth my edges like sea glass, bury me
like treasure someone might be glad to find.

PART II

A KIND OF MAGIC

I know what you've been thinking: how
does she have so much time to look out windows?

Each day offers an embarrassment
of hours for me to fill with thought

experiments and cardio, sessions
at my desk staring at the grass out back.

Yesterday a groundhog waddled across
the yard while I tried to understand

what to wear now that I'm not young.
On good days I spend hours rearranging

furniture, grateful for the strain in my quads,
the relief found in the tangible.

I know what you've been thinking—something
about women and overthinking. Something

about privilege or wasted potential.
If nothing matters, everything matters,

but still, we assign values. I don't know
how to style my hair, how to define

my purpose. In the ink-dark hours
when the house breathes heavy with sleep,

I can't see anything in the window
but my own reflection. Waiting

reveals the world outside, a sharpening
of edges. Isn't this a kind of magic?

My face morphs into blades of wild
grass, then disappears completely.

ON THE PRECIPICE

Some nights I wake up terrified of the world
our children will inherit: the rising oceans
of plastic, poisonous factory fumes, water
tainted and growing scarce. It's harder now
to be alive than it was when I was young.

Trees stand erect, as stern as prison bars.
The earth is soft under our feet, all fallen
leaves and moss. We hike for exercise, counting
our steps and calories, forgetting to
look up. Once, on a cliff's edge I believed

I could see the entire world before me, but
it was only a few miles. My son may not
have children of his own, so dim our prospects
moving on. Who can blame him? I'm useless
with abstraction, can't fathom economies

or galaxies or time. *Future* is a word
I can't grasp. The world has always been terrible
with beauty, indifferent and unattainable,
but we are ruled by greed, all sticky fingers
and grasping hands. We want and want and want,

and tell ourselves we *need*. When I was small
and home with fever, I lay on the couch, called
it my boat. I had to stay afloat, so kept
what I needed in arm's reach. But now my needs
are vast. I take five different medications

for an illness I can't see. I won't watch footage
of polar bears starving or aftermaths of bombings.
I don't check my pockets when beggars ask
for bus fare. I've grown hard, impassive—nothing
like who I thought I'd be. I wouldn't say

I'm selfish, but who admits a thing like that?
Human suffering surrounds us, but I
have deadlines, bills to pay. All the things I fear
threaten to drag me under. My son assures me
he'll be fine. His words become my lifeline.

GLOSE FOR MY SON, AFTER BISHOP'S "IN THE WAITING ROOM"

> *But I felt: you are an* I
> *you are an* Elizabeth,
> *you are one of them.*
> Why *should you be one, too?*

It's true that sometimes everything feels
like an antechamber to something else—
I've been waiting in a room stocked with magazines,
glossy suggestions of who I might have been,
of where, someday, I tell myself I'll travel.
The waiting is torture, but I try
to model patience, try not to check the clock.
The ultrasound revealed a pulsing blob, a thing
inside me, but not me. I did not cry,
but I felt: you are an *I*

a thing distinct from others
and yet—this other one inside me
waiting as I wait. How long before
our names are called, before we are summoned
or released or merely recognized?
My labor was short, your first breath—
that raspy wail—just three hours after
my water broke. Once it started, I couldn't go
back, my separateness a kind of death:
you are an Elizabeth

I told myself, and *he is not you*—but
for years your grassy scent, your chatter, tethered
me to this earth, assured me I belong. Now
you are old enough to lock your door.

Time teaches us patience for want
of an alternative, but we are all bile and phlegm
and blood pulsing with desperation.
When you were small, the heft of you restored me,
redeemed the humanity I condemned:
You are one of them—

But now I feel you leaving. Already
you reject the endless waiting, the bowing
down to a withholding world. The atlas
is your itinerary, each page
a destination. Your wanderlust inspires
advice I give us both: pursue
the things you love. Don't confuse patience
with complacency. I have been a coward
for too long, waiting, asking *What do I do?*
Why should you be one, too?

SEPTEMBER

Today my son seemed happy, and I was happy.
My husband vacuumed my car and repotted plants,
lost in the contented calm of work, and I was calm.

Alone I don't know what I feel, so I sit
outside and listen to the trees, the hustle
of their inhabitants. It is September.

Summer's distant rip of motors subsides,
its wake a silencing of human things—
white noise crowding out calculations,

fresh paint rolling over a mural of loud,
insistent colors. I see how beautiful
a blank can be, leaving me space to find

a turtle bathing in the front-yard sun,
a fox darting just beyond the fence, hummingbirds
barking, chasing mates. Today the universe

is an apple gleaming. I forget to check
for bruises. I don't concern myself with worms.
Today I just bare my crooked teeth and bite.

EPIPHANY IN THE BADLANDS

The landscape hardens like an angry face:
umber crags scrape against billowing sky
without apology for taking space.

Spires rise from volcanic fields, full of grace
and power. At home, my panic ossifies
like the landscape's hard edge. An angular face

glares back at me from my mirror, but this place
teaches me to soften. For years, a lie
that said, *Apologize for taking space*,

defined me as an error to erase,
but in this rocky plain, I amplify.
The landscape heartens me, its stoic face

insisting: *Breathe*. I've been trying to outpace
the past, as if I can escape the reasons why
I feel I must apologize for taking space,

but I don't know myself. The hot embrace
of wind against my skin, a tender sigh.
The landscape reflects my aging face.
Without apology, I take this space.

FIRST LOVE AT FOUR CORNERS

The line for photographs stretched past the fence
surrounding us. My son held our place while I

waited for water in another line that stretched
beyond my patience. The sun was hot,

the monument no more than sidewalk stones
and a seal encircling the place where four states meet.

In stalls surrounding us, Navajos sold souvenirs.
After posing for pictures, we browsed earrings.

That summer, my son's first love loomed. He chose
a pair of studs, yellow crystals. *Like the sun*,

he said. After two more days of driving, he
would catalog his doubts, reveal the nag

of wanting out, the other shoe about to drop.
But that day at Four Corners, he was at ease.

We took selfies, panting in the heat, miles
from home, in four places all at once and also

no place at all: a paved patch of dusty earth,
a flat monument to man-made boundaries.

We marveled that day at the intersection of time
and space, how far we'd come, how easy it was

to become greater than we were. That day
we transformed, simple trinkets turned to stars.

ELEGY: SHIPROCK 2021, WITH MY TEENAGE SON

We crossed through Appalachian ranges, lushly
rolling farmland that flattened to cornfields, listening
to Bowie albums all the way through, chatting
about everywhere we want, someday, to travel.

You ate a cheeseburger in every state
we crossed. My mind quieted. The northern block
of Texas was brittle and burning with August heat,
old Route 66 a lesson in entropy:

abandoned gas stations and motels, neon
signs unhinged, a twenty-foot cowboy boot
faded red and peeling. But the sky radiated
an impossible blue. The desiccated earth burned

umber, a low flame. By the time we reached New Mexico,
I could breathe. My body slackened. We stopped
by a giant crag that rose like an alien ship,
dubbed *Tsé Bit'a'í* by the Navajo,

"winged rock," though it's "Shiprock" on all the maps—
as if this weight could fly or sail away.
The contradiction moved me. I felt hope.
You felt it too, a lightening. Our lives

back home shrank until we could not remember
who we'd been before. Relief a desert breeze.
We took photographs. You left your cap on the roof
of the car, forgetting until we were miles away.

I said, *No, we can't go back.* You understood.
I think about your cap sometimes, dusty
relic of the boy you were, cradled in the arms
of a cactus or half buried in the sand.

Sometimes it is a comfort to think of it,
a token to prove we were there. Sometimes
it is a sadness, a pang of something lost.
When we speak of that place—a rock with wings, a weight

miraculously lifting—we lower
our voices as in prayer. In the pauses between
our words, those sacred intermissions, I tell
myself you know I've done the best I can.

ON A SPRING DAY, MY SON COMES TO ME DESPAIRING

Vivid pink and lilac, the thickening green
of passing time: no color I can see

doesn't promise new life, fresh blossoming.
The yellow bursts on the neighbor's forsythia mock

my dark mood. Even as the sun came up
I grieved the fragility of all I love.

The deer bounding beyond the fence will soon
be lost behind the fullness of summer leaves,

another season gone. By the time he wakes,
I've already dried my eyes. Inside, I water

the succulents, the ice plant's leaves like origami
boxes. *I just feel so alone*, he says,

his face a kind of mirror. I nod, then point
to the trailing jade. What began as cuttings, shy

and spindly sprigs, now crowd my desk with their sprawl.
I can't bear thinking of his loneliness.

Meanwhile, our cat basks in a patch of brightness,
directing us to see, after all, the light.

GLOSE FOR SARAH

> *About suffering they were never wrong,*
> *The old Masters: how well they understood*
> *Its human position: how it takes place*
> *While someone else is eating or opening a window or just walking dully along*
>   —W. H. Auden, "Musée des Beaux Arts"

And what good are condolences? You've known
for decades tragedy's indifference. You recognize
the sound of your daughter's keening as the sound
you made when your own father died, but now
you swallow your sobs, your face a wall
crumbling. Some cultures ritualize their grief, call it song
and find some comfort there. You took comfort
in your father's ashes, sleeping with them for a week,
but how much can one person bear and for how long?
About suffering they were never wrong,

the doctors who used words like *inoperable*,
aggressive. Your Virgo brain held fast to regimens.
He wouldn't have lived so long without my care.
And even as the morphine drip failed to mute
his agony, he raged with you over injustices.
Fuck racism, fuck cancer. Your children, who would,
like you, be fatherless, are light enough to pass,
their features more yours than his, but still—
their ancestors bore chains, feared the white hood,
the old Masters. How well they understood

loss and injustice and suffering. The day after
he died, you were already choosing granite
for his headstone. You flipped through samples,
the absurdity of Bahama Blue, Apache Red, Canadian Green

eliciting a bitter laugh, even in the throes of grief,
your humor sharp as scalpels. *Imagine his face,*
you said, *if he knew the one I chose: American Black.*
But isn't this the point? He would never know this or
his children grown or anything again—and what of grace?
Its human position? How it takes place

only briefly and then falls away. How you learn
to accept its disappearance, spend a lifetime waiting
for its return. You've been staying up too late,
packing boxes. You've rearranged the furniture just enough
so that his absence isn't the only change; you need
something else to be different. You tell me, *Strong
has nothing to do with it.* Your face, pale stone,
is still so young. *The kids need me. I have no choice.*
And so you carry on, in spite of all that's wrong,
while someone else is eating or opening a window or just walking dully along.

LATE SEPTEMBER IN DRUID HILL PARK

It is barely afternoon, but the owl's questions
fill the woods, pensive and incongruous.

Deer haunt my peripheries, I know from the sounds
of their movement. It's the kind of day we dream about

in the dank oppression of August, skin sticking
to skin, thirsty for cooler air. Was it just a week ago

a violence of wind brought down twin oaks?
A week ago a shattering resounded

through the nave? Her mother's wails. I hadn't been
to church in years. No one belongs at the funeral

of a child. I looked at my hands poised in my lap
like someone else's hands. At home, I held my son

until he pulled away. Today is calm, quiet
save the dead leaves crunching underfoot,

the songbirds' anxious chatter, the owl's
plaintive calling: *So soon? So soon? So soon?*

DANCE CLASS

Though the sky is gray like timeworn sheets, spring colors
assert themselves: bold dancers swirling scarves

as in the dank church rec room where I hid
behind my mother, frowning at the box

of gauzy polyester: peach and purple,
fuchsia and teal, the other girls already

waving the strips of fabric as instructed,
the room a kaleidoscope exploding. Now,

as then, I root in place, the world unfurling
as I watch and wait. In another week, my view

will be obscured, foliage thickening, the pink
of the cherry tree replaced by sturdy green.

Of all the things I fail to understand,
time vexes me the most. I am both here—

stumbling through middle age, still uneasy
in my body, keeping mostly to myself—

and there, still hiding, watching other girls dance.
Then, as now, I found my place: backed against

the wall of this indifferent world, mesmerized
by so much movement, such violence of color.

LISTENING TO SPOTIFY ON THE RIDE TO SCHOOL, WINTER 2021

The percussion is a clucking tongue—wooden
mallets on a rhythm block like the toy instruments

he played when he was just a boy, when his kit
was pots and pans. Now he towers over me,

his promise fierce, ambition pulsing through him,
but he doesn't see the light slanting through

the stand of leafless trees, the way those rays
illuminate everything I've ever lost

or wanted, doesn't know the cruel tricks time
will play, how easy it becomes to lose

oneself to life's endless distractions, how
we must learn patience over and over until

we slow down enough to see what is before us,
and even then, nothing stays unchanged for long.

Look—even the concrete storage facility
is dignified in this morning light, something

to mourn when clouds roll in and the sky is no longer
cold rivers. In this moment I might believe

I can protect him from disappointment. I might
believe the least of us can be redeemed.

At school, he pauses, puts in his earbuds, adjusts
his face to an impassive mask. My son,

who knows already the armor we must wear
against the world. Who's known for years how music,

at best, is more than the sum of its parts. I want
to tell him this holds true for each of us.

I want forgiveness for all I am not.
I wait to cry until I'm heading south.

The light, having advanced, now blinds the drivers,
slowing our collective pace, but still, we weave

too fast from lane to lane. I've been in a hurry
all my life. The whole way home is stop and go,

a stuttering to my exit. When I arrive,
I will set to my daily work, my mind abuzz

with old frequencies, but a new thought moving me:
if light could speak, then surely it would sing.

PATHETIC FALLACY

The sky is neither wound nor bruise nor gash.
It is not fabric tearing open. Light
does not move with violence; it radiates.
It is we who are brazen or uncanny,
sublime or broken.   Yesterday morning
a turtle blocked the street outside my house.
I moved her to the sidewalk. By afternoon
she blocked my driveway. I moved her to the lawn.
She stayed so long in the shaggy grass I
checked twice to see if she was dead, but she
recoiled at my touch. I googled terraria,
turtle diets, basking lights. I made a list
of names, but in the morning she was gone.

I keep looking to the sky to tell me how
I feel. Not even five o'clock and a vague
darkness closes in. Deer disappear
into the woods save the blinking white of their tails.
Meanwhile upstairs the dryer clanks. The fretting
buzz of human busyness surrounds me,
droning traffic white noise to help me sleep.

Daylight always comes again unprompted,
promising another chance. How I long
to emulate this faithfully spinning planet,
its endless graceful falling toward the sun.

THE DEER

I saw my anger tripping up the hill
out back, into the forest, a fawn wobbling.
I didn't believe it either at first—that such

a bitter thing as rage could be so young,
so clumsy—I reminded myself to breathe,
feeling confident in each inhalation.

I was glad to see her go. My body slackened.
The world unfolded like a map inviting
exploration. I don't know how to measure

my own state of mind, but I see my anger
nibbling foliage behind our backyard fence.
The distance between us is a garden, wild

with weeds and native grasses. What kind of fury
feeds on leaves? But there she is. Her eyes are
cartoon-big, question-batting buttons. She looks

in my direction, but I've made myself
invisible, and therefore, I'm convinced,
impervious to her. In the morning, though,

she's jumped the fence back in. Older, her spots
have molted to tawny brown. She is devouring
the strawberries in my garden. I feel her tense,

wait for her to bolt, but she stills, looks up.
We stare at each other through my office window.
An epiphany: she is afraid. My anger

too afraid to move! Do I tell her everything's
okay? Do I grab hold of her hide to shake her?
Look around you! I could shout. *The light refracts*

*like disco sparkle. The hours already slip
away. There is no time for all this drama,
my trembling little deer.* But I say nothing.

I could shoo her away but instead we halt
in stalemate staring. I memorize her doe-
eyed face with blooming warmth akin to love.

GLOSE FOR FATHERS

> *Speaking indifferently to him,*
> *who had driven out the cold*
> *and polished my good shoes as well.*
> *What did I know, what did I know*
>   —Robert Hayden's "Those Winter Sundays"

What I mean to say is that all fathers
bear the burden of their children's
blame. Bedtime stories promised us
protection, but gave no guidance
about dangers we brought on ourselves.
How could he save us from every whim
to fight or steal or dull the edges with
this shot, that pill? And yet our anger
bubbled. We were disasters, spitting at the brim,
speaking indifferently to him

to hide our hurt. Shall we catalogue
our grievances? Did one concern money?
Lack of attention? Lack of love?
Did we sense we were not good enough?
Against the brick wall, he held me,
eyes sharp with fear, in a chokehold
to save me from my own flailing fury,
his hand around my throat more embrace
than assault. My father, suddenly old,
who had driven out the cold

for me and taught me the physics required
to move through time and space,
had never held me with such force

before. I'll take this as a kind of love.
What I mean to say is how can we
know what circumstances may compel
a man to act? For years, I'd been part
of the audience, his presence like a poster.
I ironed my best dress, as under a spell,
and polished my good shoes as well,

for each performance, desperate to catch
his eye. What I mean is a person can feel
two things at once, a doubled blade
not quite enough to cut us off completely.
Trumpet in hand, his silence was not slight;
he had to save his breath. His tuxedo,
frayed cuffs, patched elbows, did not
signify the choice I once believed.
He played his part, show after show.
What did I know? What did I know?

WAITING FOR BATS
Returning to Laceyville after Twenty Years

For a week of dusks, I sit on the porch waiting
for the bats. Twenty years ago, they came

like clockwork as the sky obscured to purple.
They were unafraid of me, darting so close

I captured one with a click of my old Nikon;
in the print she is a glow-eyed blur with webbed wings.

But twenty years later, none come. Twenty years
is long enough for patterns to shift, for one marriage

to end and another to begin, for a child
to be born and grow, almost, into a man.

It was August then, not June. As the sun sets,
I see rabbits and chipmunks, a groundhog thudding

across the yard, swallows swooping left and right,
the whole world changing color. Sometimes we

don't know what we're waiting for until it comes
to us: the scamper and squawk of wildlife,

the way darkness grows so gradually, your eyes
adjust and you see spectrums in the nighttime.

The air has gotten a little cool, opening
like a window in a stuffy room. I forget

I was worried about money and time. I am attuned
to movement, but still the bats don't come. By the end

of the week, my expectations fade away,
a freedom I will try to carry with me.

RETREAT

The air out here is clean and easy, cool
for this deep into June. The deer seem different, too—
frolicking through open fields denied the deer
who live behind my house. This, and the wavering
yellow grasses that shimmer in the falling
light, help me forget myself. I keep waiting to feel

like a grown-up, to quell my knee-jerk jealousies,
my fury over inevitable change, my impossible
ambitions. I try to read the recipe
for peace in the faces of older women, but none
can tell me how far away I need to stand
to see my life more clearly. I keep leaving

the small white church where I've been staying, hoping
to walk out of this anxious loneliness.
The more I walk the brighter I feel, less hazy
around the edges. I'm expansive in this light.
The whirligigs still sparkle in the sun,
just as they did twenty years ago when I walked

this same dirt road. The kids who live in the trailer
up the hill watch me warily, my flannel shirt tied
like a cape around my shoulders. I'm learning to love
this aimlessness, surrendering to the curve
in the road. So much of this life is a circling back,
each act an echo fading in the valley.

GLOSE AFTER SESHADRI'S "CLIFFHANGING"

>*I won't let myself fall, but I don't want to pull myself up.*
>*I'm ambivalent. I'm ambivalent forever now.*
>*But if you were here, looking down on me and saying,*
>*"Grab my hand, grab my hand," I would, I know, I surely would.*
>   —Vijay Seshadri's "Cliffhanging"

This morning you told me you don't care
about feeling better anymore: you've adapted
to the nagging doom, the dirt we brush beneath
the carpet, the other shoe that always drops.
I'd say you're too young to be so dark, but
when I was your age, sadness and rage were mixed up
in everything I felt, vibrations holding me together.
You see my inconsistencies. I embrace my despair
as an old friend, even as I insist you must *fill your own cup*;
I won't let myself fall, but I don't want to pull myself up.

I've tried to hide my uncertainty, but you winced
when I said the best years are ahead, so now
I say time and age teach you to fall a little less
painfully. I say skin thins as you get older, so steel
yourself against disappointments now, practice breathing,
learn your limits, trust discerningly, don't allow
your inner critic to stifle every effort. I know it's hard,
but some days just going through the motions
is its own accomplishment; I'm still learning how.
I'm ambivalent. I'm ambivalent forever now

about everything except endorphins and rising
seas and time moving in one direction, with
or without us. It's not an easy moment to be alive.

You hear me shout at other drivers, curse my rivals,
declare I can't do it anymore. I don't know
whether everyone feels this way—that staying
in one place will do them in. I've fallen apart
before your eyes, madwoman on her knees.
I've failed to model gratitude, patience, praying—
but if you were here, looking down on me and saying,

I don't believe in anything either, I'd force myself
to stand. I'd show you, tattooed on my arm:
There are millions of suns left. Some days this optimism
is more grimace than smile, but still—I've papered
my office with verses I love, photographs of people
I love, a stack of books—the armor of my adulthood.
It's easy to turn bitter, to ignore the miraculous beating heart,
the sun's bold assertions. But if you fell, I'd call out,
Get up, keep going (I have a whole arsenal of good),
Grab my hand, grab my hand. I would, I know, I surely would.

DRIVING MY SON HOME FROM THE TATTOO PARLOR

1.
The thin black outline of a star swells pink
beneath the bandage on your wrist. The weather
is a split screen: sunlight to the west, bright
and yellow; to the east a purple smudge of cloud.
Drops pelt the windshield uncertainly. You look up
from your phone and gape: iridescence splashes
from traffic, tires kicking up spectrums of color
like video game graphics, psychedelic trails
swirling at high speed. When we reach our exit
we see the wide, low arc stretched over the city,
a postcard rainbow we deem a hopeful sign.

2.
You can't wait to take the bandage off, for the skin
to scab and heal, for your life to begin somewhere else,
somewhere with desert and mountains, a place
where you feel free. I know you know most wounds
don't heal so easily. More often we make do
despite discomfort, glaring scars, unsettled
scores. I've tried to learn to want things
as they are, and some days I remember how.

3.
We used to read a picture book in which
a crocodile collected puddles. Nothing
stayed as he wanted, reflections altering
as he moved, but with the water he painted pictures,
and when the pail was empty, he used it to catch
shadows. What I mean to say is I try

to hold these moments, contain somehow the hours
in the car or at the counter in our kitchen
where you do homework and complain about
various indignities of being alive.

4.
In a year or five or twenty, will you regret
the star on your wrist? Will you remember the drive
and the rainbow and the rain? When you were small
I gave you crayons and paper, instruments
and songs. What can I give you now? A map
to guide you away from here? Impermanence
and chaos will follow you, but
you know this already. The days are growing
short again, darkness draped over us when we wake,
but spring will come back, bringing better light.
The light is always shifting, but the sky
through everything contains spectrums and stars.
Constant and merciful, the sky will hold.

I DON'T BELIEVE IN MAGIC

but as we approach the summit, sky expands
to fill the space between thinning leaves, creating

verdant lace against a blue expanse. What I mean
is everything changes. We see only distance:

sky and patchwork fields dotted with barns and silos,
rows of corn like stripes, the highway that brought us here.

The further we hiked from the parking lot, the easier
I breathed, anxieties giving way to wordless

wonder. It's good to see how everything fits
together, to see such vistas exist outside

screensavers and postcards. We look in silence,
passing an apple back and forth, our crunching

and the chittering birds and the wind a kind of music.
That's all. Nothing happens. We know we can't capture

the scope of the landscape, but we take pictures anyway.
Years later we'll scroll through images, marvel

at how young we were, transported back to mingle
with ghosts of kindred travelers. *Remember?* we'll say.

How the world became a gesture inviting us in.
How we sat together at the edge thinking, *Yes*.

SUCH WONDERS
2 a.m., Coming home from the emergency room

On the boat, before your accident, we killed
the motor and waited for a green flare:
when the sun hits the tip of a mountain's highest peak,
emerald bursting like a science fiction time warp.

Our eyes grew raw from staring at the sun,
but nothing happened. Still, it was beautiful
the way the sky took on a golden tinge
and the water was almost glowing. Such wonders

reveal themselves every day. In Cuba our tour guide
plucked passion fruit from the vine, its flesh tart
as the bite of an angry kiss. Didn't we marvel
at the sweetness? Our children were so young back then.

Time expands like hot metal we're too afraid
to touch. I've cradled the corpses of butterflies,
wings intricate as cathedral windows,
delicate as old parchment. I've opened stones

to find trilobites, the tidiness of their hiding
a miraculous magic trick. Even grass grows
right before our eyes. Last week I learned that lightning
travels underground when I saw the white oak

burned up from its roots. It's good to be reminded
of how much I still don't know, to be shocked into
awareness as we seek relief from humid
summers in a lake so cold it steals our breath.

I didn't see what happened when you fell.
You've stepped from boat to dock a hundred times
before; it was just a stupid accident,
a broken rib and thirteen stitches—nothing

that would not heal, but all night I was angry
at the fragility of your body, the split-
second missteps that cannot be undone.
Fatigue pixelated the night, grainy black

and white, like old TV. On the road home,
I stopped in time to let a trio of raccoons
dash past and disappear into the woods.
By then, we were giddy with our own survival.

So much disaster looms on the peripheries,
but back at the lake fireflies pulsed,
their slowly growing lights a comfort: for every
flare that faded out, another one lit up.

ACKNOWLEDGMENTS

Many thanks to the following publications in which these poems first appeared:

Atticus Review: "Elegy: Shiprock 2021"
EPOCH: "Margin of Error"
failbetter: "Panic"
On the Seawall: "Hell's Half Acre"
Smartish Pace: "Glose after Seshadri's 'Cliffhanging'"
The Common: "Real Estate for the Blended Family"
The Hopkins Review: "Glose for My Son, after Bishop's 'In the Waiting Room'" and "Glose for Fathers"
The MacGuffin: "Second Marriage," "Mercy," "Whelm"
The Shore Poetry: "Approximations"

THANKS

Thank you to Courtney LeBlanc and the Riot in Your Throat team for giving this collection a home and making the process of bringing it into the world such a pleasure.

Thank you to Rose Solari and Jimmy Patterson for your continued belief in and support of my work. You were there at the very beginning, and I am so grateful for your steady presence in my life.

Thank you to the Soaring Gardens Artists Retreat. My time there allowed me to finish a draft of this manuscript.

Thank you to the literary community of Baltimore for giving me such a warm and welcoming home, especially the fine folks at the Ivy Bookshop, *BmoreArt Magazine*, and Good Contrivance Farm: Nicole Allen, Nate Brown, Rita Collins, Michael Downs, Hannah Fenster, Amani Jackson, Chelsea Lemon Fetzer, Cara Ober, Emma Snyder, Ron Tanner, Khaliah Williams, and the many other bright, creative people who make me fall in love over and over again with this city's grit and charm.

Thank you to my generous early readers and supportive friends: Don Berger, Jessica Anya Blau, Steve Bolton, Betsy Boyd, Elisabeth Dahl, Jane Delury, Kathy Flann, Lindsay Fleming, Paris Goudas, Christine Grillo, Don Lee, Steven Leyva, Elizabeth Lunt, James Magruder, Jane Satterfield, Marion Winik, and Sarah Woodruff. I am lucky to know you.

Thank you to my brother, Benjamin Hazen. You inspire me with your dedication, imagination, and skill. And thank you to our parents, Robert and Margaret Hazen, for showing us the creative path early and supporting our efforts for all these years.

Thank you to my son, Greg Ehrhardt. You are the reason for so many of these poems.

And thank you to my husband, Grantley Pyke, for sticking around through the darker days so we can enjoy the light together.

ABOUT THE AUTHOR

Elizabeth Hazen is a poet and essayist whose work has appeared in *The Best American Poetry*, *Epoch*, *Fourth Genre*, *Southwest Review*, the *Threepenny Review*, the *Normal School*, and other journals. She's the author of the full-length collections *Chaos Theories*, *Girls Like Us*, and *The Sky Will Hold*. She lives in Baltimore with her family. Find her online at www.elizabethhazen.com.

ABOUT THE PRESS

Riot in Your Throat is an independent press that publishes fierce, feminist poetry.

Support independent authors, artists, and presses.

Visit us online:
www.riotinyourthroat.com

RIOT IN YOUR THROAT BOOKS

Sarah Beddow   *Dispatches from Frontier Schools*
Kathryn Bratt-Pfotenhauer   *Bad Animal*
Kimberly Casey   *Where the Water Begins*
Sonia Greenfield   *All Possible Histories*
Elizabeth Hazen   *The Sky Will Hold*
Brett Elizabeth Jenkins   *Brilliant Little Body*
Melissa Fite Johnson   *Green*
Melissa Fite Johnson   *Midlife Abecedarian*
Hadley Jones   *Devout*
Hilary King   *Stitched on Me*
Frances Klein   *Another Life*
Courtney LeBlanc   *Exquisite Bloody, Beating Heart*
Courtney LeBlanc   *Her Dark Everything*
Jill Michelle   *Underwater*
Shilo Niziolek   *Little Deaths*
Laura Passin   *Borrowing Your Body*
Laura Passin   *We the Destroyers*
Sara Quinn Rivara   *Little Beast*
Laurie Rachkus Uttich   *Somewhere, a Woman Lowers the Hem of Her Skirt*
Karen J. Weyant   *Avoiding the Rapture*

www.ingramcontent.com/pod-product-compliance
Lightning Source LLC
LaVergne TN
LVHW041627070526
838199LV00052B/3268